SONIA SOTOMAYOR

FIRST HISPANIC U.S. SUPREME COURT JUSTICE

SONIA SOTOMAYOR

FIRST HISPANIC U.S. SUPREME COURT JUSTICE

Lisa Tucker McElroy

LERNER PUBLICATIONS COMPANY · MINNEAPOLIS

This book is for Zoe and Abby McElroy. If Sonia Sotomayor can make it, then you can too!

The images in this book are used with the permission of: AP Photo/Collection of the Supreme Court of the United States, Steve Petteway, pp. 2, 35; © Jim Young/Reuters/ CORBIS, p. 6; AP Photo/Ricardo Arduengo, p. 8; AP Photo/White House, pp. 9, 10, 12, 14, 17, 21; © CBS Photo Archive/Hulton Archive/Getty Images, p. 11; AP Photo/Eddie Adams, p. 13; © Spencer Platt/Getty Images, p. 15; AP Photo, p. 16; Photo: Princeton University, Office of Communications, p. 18; © age fotostock/SuperStock, p. 19; AP Photo/David A. Cantor, p. 22; AP Photo/Ron Frehm, p. 23; AP Photo/Adam Nadel, File, p. 25; AP Photo/Mark Lennihan, File, p. 26; © Saul Loeb/AFP/Getty Images, p. 27; AP Photo/Manuel Balce Ceneta, p. 28; AP Photo/Pablo Martinez Monsivais, pp. 29, 33; AP Photo/Charles Dharapak, pp. 30, 36 (bottom); © Michael McCloskey/Photodisc/Getty Images, p. 34; AP Photo/J. Scott Applewhite, p. 36 (top); © Abby Brack/Getty Images, p. 38; © Miguel Rajmil/EFE/ZUMA Press, p. 39; AP Photo/Ron Edmonds, p. 40.
Front cover: © Stacey Ilyse Photography/The White House via Getty Images.

Lerner Publications Company
A division of Lerner Publishing Group, Inc.
241 First Avenue North
Minneapolis, MN 55401 U.S.A.

Website address: www.lernerbooks.com

Library of Congress Cataloging-in-Publication Data

McElroy, Lisa Tucker.
    Sonia Sotomayor : first Hispanic U.S. Supreme Court justice / by Lisa Tucker McElroy.
        p.   cm. — (Gateway biographies)
    Includes bibliographical references and index.
    ISBN 978-0-7613-5861-9 (lib. bdg. : alk. paper)
    1. Sotomayor, Sonia, 1954– 2. Hispanic American judges—Biography. 3. Judges— United States—Biography. I. Title.
    KF8745.S68M34 2010
    347.73'2634—dc22 [B]   2009037703

Manufactured in the United States of America
1 – BP – 12/15/09

CONTENTS

Sonia Sotomayor *(left)* takes the oath of office on August 8, 2009. John Roberts *(right)*, chief justice of the United States, administers the oath. Sotomayor's mother, Celina, holds the Bible while her brother, Juan, looks on.

Many Americans had looked forward to this day for years. A dark-haired woman stood next to her mother and brother in a marble room in Washington, D.C. Her left hand was on a Bible. The chief justice, wearing his black robes, read the oath of office. In this special ceremony on August 8, 2009, Sonia Sotomayor became the first Hispanic justice of the U.S. Supreme Court.

Childhood

Sonia Sotomayor was born in the Bronx (a part of New York City) on June 25, 1954. She was the first person in her family to be born in the continental United States. Her parents, Celina and Juan Sotomayor, were from Puerto Rico, a U.S. island off the coast of Florida. Celina grew up poor in the farming community of Lajas, Puerto Rico. Later, she often told her friends that she and her four siblings had only one pencil to share. They

Sonia Sotomayor's mother, Celina, grew up in the Santa Rosa neighborhood of Lajas, Puerto Rico, shown here in 2009.

took turns using it to do their homework. At seventeen, during World War II (1939–1945), Celina joined the Women's Army Corps (WAC). She left Puerto Rico, speaking very little English, and arrived in Georgia in 1944 to begin training.

After Celina's service in the WAC, she met and married Juan Sotomayor, a machinist, who had also grown up poor in Puerto Rico. The couple moved to New York City. There Celina worked as a hospital telephone operator. Juan and Celina lived in a public housing project in the

Bronx because they did not have much money. While living there, they had two children—Sonia and her younger brother, Juan. The family did not speak English at home because Sonia's father spoke only Spanish. Her parents worked very hard to make a good life for their kids.

Sonia as a baby with her mother, Celina, and father, Juan. The family lived in the Bronx in New York City.

10

Sonia at the age of six or seven. Her father died just a few years later.

Sonia's father died from heart problems when she was only nine years old. After he died, Sonia started speaking more English at home. Although Sonia had been fluent in English before, her English-language skills grew even stronger. Sonia loved to read, and becoming more comfortable with English meant that she could read English-language books more easily. Her favorites were the Nancy Drew mystery series, about a girl detective. After reading about Nancy's adventures, Sonia decided that she wanted to be a detective too. She also read comic books about Archie and Richie Rich. Celina bought Sonia and Juan a set of *Encyclopaedia Britannica* books. They were the only family in their neighborhood to have a set. Celina struggled to make the payments on the books, but she wanted her children to learn. She often told her children, "I do not care what you do, but be the best at it."

As a child, Sonia was not always healthy. When she was eight years old, doctors said she had diabetes. This disease affects how the body uses sugar. She began taking shots of insulin, a medicine that helped her body work better. Sonia had to give herself shots every day. This was no fun, and she would need to give herself the shots for the rest of her life. Sonia was told that detective work wouldn't be realistic for her. She decided that she wanted to be an attorney and a judge instead. She had become a big fan of *Perry Mason*, a TV courtroom drama popular during the 1960s. From watching the

The TV show *Perry Mason* was one of Sonia's favorites when she was a child. Here actors Raymond Burr and Barbara Hale play a lawyer and his secretary in an episode from 1959.

show, she has said, "I realized that the judge was the most important player in the room." She has also said, "I was going to college and I was going to become an attorney, and I knew that when I was ten. No jest."

Sonia also liked to go to the movies with her cousins. Family parties were fun as well. Her family played merengue (Latin dance) music and ate Puerto Rican dishes such as roast pork and beans.

Sonia fought to protect others even as a child. Her brother remembers that she helped him when older

boys tried to mug him in the neighborhood where they first lived. "If I had a kid picking on me," Juan has said, "she would try to negotiate. If she couldn't, she would move on to step two. She could mix it up [fight if she had to]."

Sonia loved to attend parties with her family when she was young.

The Sotomayors lived in Co-Op City in the Bronx, shown here in 1977. Co-Op City is the largest cooperative housing development in the world.

When Sonia was in middle school, her family moved to Co-Op City. This apartment complex was a step up from their former neighborhood. In Co-Op City, Celina took the smaller of the two bedrooms and divided the larger one for Sonia and Juan. Celina studied for her nurse's license and began working as a nurse. Many times neighborhood friends would go to her for help.

Sonia is shown here in her cap and gown when she graduated from eighth grade. She worked hard in school but also liked hanging out with her friends.

After working long hours, Celina would come home to find Sonia and Juan and many of their friends hanging out together. The Sotomayor home was a fun place to be. Celina often cooked rice, beans, and pork chops for everyone.

High school was not always an easy time for Sonia, but her mother helped guide her through. Many teens in Sonia's neighborhood used drugs. She still remembers seeing drug dealers in the hallways of her apartment building. Sonia knew she had to stay away from drugs, so she found other ways to fill her time. She worked at a local store and at a hospital. She was also involved in student government and in the debate club. And she had a good group of friends—including a steady boyfriend named Kevin Noonan.

She liked to play bingo on Saturday nights with her friends and family. They used chickpeas as markers. Kids who knew her then said that she was always friendly and popular, bright and lively. She made time for them and made them feel important.

Sonia always studied hard. She was one of the best students in her high school class. Sonia was named class valedictorian when she graduated in 1972 from Cardinal Spellman High School in the Bronx.

Sonia attended Cardinal Spellman High School in the Bronx. The school is shown here in 2009.

College and Law School

Sonia decided to go to Princeton University, in Princeton, New Jersey. It is one of the best colleges in the country. She did so well in high school that Princeton gave her a full scholarship (an award that pays for college fees). She didn't have to pay college tuition at all.

In her early days at Princeton, she was very scared. She barely raised her hand in class. There weren't many Hispanic people at Princeton in those days. Looking back, she has said that she felt like "a visitor landing in an alien country." She quickly made friends, though, and she started to feel as if she fit in.

Sotomayor attended Princeton University in New Jersey, shown here in 1970.

Sotomayor in a photo from the 1976 Princeton yearbook. In the yearbook, Sotomayor thanked all the people she had met at the school for their "lessons of life."

While she was in college, Sonia studied very hard and earned good grades. She was a history major, so many of her classes involved reading and writing. Writing was not easy for her, in part because English was her second language. She often read grammar and writing texts during her summer vacation, and she asked professors for help. She quickly improved and earned the respect of her teachers.

During her free time, she loved to go salsa dancing with friends. She also began an after-school program for local children and volunteered as an interpreter for Hispanic patients at Trenton Psychiatric Hospital. To pay for books, she babysat for her godson. She even bought him G.I. Joe dolls to play with in her dorm room.

Sonia remembered her Puerto Rican roots. At Princeton she wrote a thesis (a long paper) about Puerto Rico's political and economic struggles. Her paper was excellent—just like all her other college work.

Sotomayor is shown here at Princeton, where she won the Pyne Prize, the university's highest award for an undergraduate.

In 1976, Sonia graduated from Princeton summa cum laude, or with highest honors. She was also awarded the Pyne Prize at graduation. This prize goes to one or more graduating seniors who have earned strong grades and demonstrated leadership skills. It is Princeton's highest undergraduate award.

That same year brought two more big events. In the summer, she married Kevin Noonan, her high school sweetheart. She also entered Yale Law School in New Haven, Connecticut. Law school was hard work. Luckily, Sonia's grades had earned her a full scholarship to Yale, just as they had at Princeton. She could focus on her studies without worrying about the costs.

In law school, Sonia had to read about many cases that U.S. courts had decided. She also had to learn about how the states and federal government made laws. She had to read and write for many hours every day. But Sonia came to love the law. She was interested in how judges worked and how lawyers could seek justice. Her professors noticed her skill and passion for the law. Her classmates said that she had a lot of self-confidence. "She would stand up for herself and not be intimidated by anyone," one classmate has said.

Sonia remained proud of her Puerto Rican heritage. At Yale she wrote a paper about Puerto Rico's quest to become a state. She also hung out with other Hispanic people at Yale, both students and staff. They enjoyed watching baseball games and dancing the salsa.

Sonia served as an editor on the *Yale Law Journal*. This is a magazine with articles about important legal issues, published by students. Being an editor on the journal was an honor, but it meant that Sonia had to work long hours. She also led the minority students' group on campus. By the time she graduated from law school in 1979, she was well prepared for the challenge of practicing law.

Sotomayor attended Yale Law School in Connecticut. She was editor of the *Yale Law Journal.*

Legal Career

After Sonia Sotomayor graduated from Yale Law School, she began working as an assistant district attorney in New York County. Her husband was doing graduate work at Princeton, and they lived near the university. She traveled the two hours one way to New York every day.

As an assistant district attorney, Sotomayor's duties included sending shoplifters, robbers, and murderers to jail. She had to work long hours, because she wanted to be sure that only people who were truly guilty of crimes went to prison. She spent many weeks—sometimes months—learning about and investigating each case. She then went to court to convince a judge and jury that the person had committed the crime. Many people said that Sotomayor was always prepared for her cases. She was a respected and admired district attorney, and she helped to put many criminals in jail.

Around this time, Sotomayor and her husband divorced. They had no children. She stayed close to her family and enjoyed spending time with her godchildren.

After five years at the district attorney's office, Sotomayor was hired by Pavia and Harcourt, a small law firm in Manhattan. She enjoyed practicing a different kind of law there, and she was eager to learn how to do a good job. Sotomayor was in the unit that worked to protect client companies' products, ideas, and designs. The companies were worried that others would try to copy their products. One company she helped was Fendi,

Sotomayor and her nephews, Conner and Corey Sotomayor, attend a baseball game at Yankee Stadium.

a firm that makes expensive handbags. The company wanted to stop people from copying its designs to make cheaper, fake Fendi handbags. Sotomayor even rode on a motorcycle with police officers who arrested people selling fake handbags in New York's Chinatown. She did such a good job that Pavia and Harcourt decided to make her a partner. This meant that she shared in the firm's profits and responsibilities.

Especially important to Sotomayor was her pro bono work. This is work that lawyers do for free. Most lawyers offer free legal services to some people who cannot afford them, but Sotomayor's pro bono work

Spectators wave flags at the annual Puerto Rican Day Parade in New York City in 1990. Sotomayor makes helping people in the Puerto Rican community a priority.

was special to her. Even with her busy schedule, she worked to help the Puerto Rican community. She tried to show immigrants how they could succeed in life, just as she had. She was on the board of the State of New York Mortgage Agency, where she worked to make housing affordable for people who did not have much money. She also helped with the Development School for Youth program. It teaches inner-city kids about future jobs. Her favorite part was the mock trial of Goldilocks and the Three Bears, where she helped kids learn what it means to be a lawyer.

Becoming a Judge

In 1992 President George H. W. Bush nominated Sotomayor to be a federal district judge in the Southern District of New York. Sotomayor was thrilled that her childhood dreams were coming true. She would finally be "the most important person in the courtroom." Sotomayor was also the youngest judge in her district and the first Hispanic judge in New York.

As a federal judge in New York, Sotomayor heard many important cases. In 1994 Major League Baseball (MLB) players went on strike. For about eight months, all MLB games were canceled because the players and owners argued about players' salaries and rights. As a baseball fan, Sotomayor was both nervous and excited when she was the judge in that case. She wanted to end the 232-day strike. With a smile, she said, "You can't

Baseball commissioner Bud Selig *(left)* and Len Coleman, president of the National League of Major League Baseball, are shown in 1995. Sotomayor dealt with baseball players and owners while handling the case involving the MLB strike as a federal judge.

grow up in the South Bronx without knowing about baseball." Sotomayor persuaded the owners to deal more fairly with the players, and baseball games resumed. For months many people called her the Savior of Baseball.

Most people found Sotomayor to be a fair but tough judge. Lawyers were always prepared when they came to her courtroom. They knew that she would have studied their cases very well and would ask them difficult questions about them.

As a judge, Sotomayor worked closely with her law clerks. These young lawyers helped her research cases and write opinions (documents that explain a judge's decision in a court case). She was a demanding boss and often kept her law clerks close by so they could help her quickly. She was also kind and caring and treated her clerks with respect. She was interested in their families and hobbies. Sotomayor would often eat lunch with her law clerks, and she made sure that she was friends with them. She attended many of her clerks' weddings and keeps pictures of them and their families in her office.

In 1997 President Bill Clinton nominated her to the U.S. Court of Appeals. Sotomayor was excited about the honor and the chance to step up to the next federal court. Her nomination had to be approved by the U.S. Senate. She faced a long hearing, where she had to answer many questions. But she proved to the senators that she would be a fair and honest judge. She became an appeals judge in 1998.

In 1999 Sotomayor started teaching a course at Columbia University Law School in New York City while she served on the court of appeals. During her ten years on the appeals court, Sotomayor heard more than three thousand cases and wrote 380 papers outlining the opinions of the majority of the appeals judges. She became the informal social chairperson of the court, organizing after-work get-togethers for her coworkers.

In a much-discussed case, Sotomayor and two other appeals court judges decided that the city of New Haven, Connecticut, had been fair when it set aside the results of a test for the promotion of firefighters. White firefighters, as a group, had scored higher on the test than

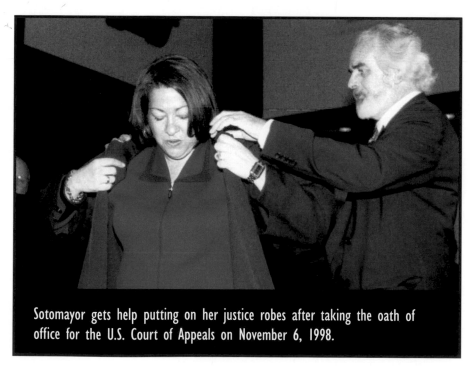

Sotomayor gets help putting on her justice robes after taking the oath of office for the U.S. Court of Appeals on November 6, 1998.

Sotomayor poses near the window in her office in New York City in 1998, after she became an appeals court judge.

most minorities. The city decided that the test should not matter. The Supreme Court would later disagree with Sotomayor and over-turn the decision in this case.

Nomination to the Supreme Court

On April 27, 2009, President Barack Obama contacted Sotomayor and told her that he might want to nominate her to the Supreme Court of the United States. President Obama told Sotomayor that the New York senators had urged him to pick her. They pointed out that she had done a great job in New York courts.

On May 26, President Obama officially announced that he was nominating Sonia Sotomayor to the Supreme Court. She would replace Justice David Souter, who had retired.

When she accepted the president's nomination,

Sotomayor said, "Eleven years ago, during my confirmation process for appointment to the Second Circuit, I was given a private tour of the White House. It was an overwhelming experience for a kid from the South Bronx. Never in my wildest childhood imaginings did I ever envision that moment, let alone . . . dream that I would live this moment." Many senators and governors immediately supported Sotomayor. They praised her past work. But other senators and governors did not support her. They believed that her Hispanic background might cause her to make decisions to benefit Hispanic people.

Sotomayor speaks at the press conference where Vice President Joe Biden *(left)* and President Barack Obama *(right)* announced her nomination for the Supreme Court.

The Confirmation Hearings

Before she took a seat on the Supreme Court, Sotomayor had to be confirmed by the Senate. She met with senators in their offices. She explained to them her views about being a judge. In fact, she was so active visiting senators that she broke her ankle on her way to visit one senator. The injury didn't stop her. Only hours after she left the hospital with a cast and crutches, she went to another meeting. One senator even signed her cast.

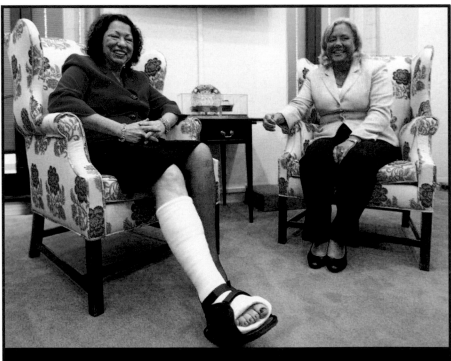

Sotomayor wears a cast on her leg during her meeting with Louisiana senator Mary Landrieu in June 2009.

Sotomayor is sworn in before testifying in front of the Senate Judiciary Committee in July 2009.

Sotomayor also had to appear before the whole Senate to answer questions. On July 13, 2009, she began the Senate hearings. During the next three days, Sotomayor sat before the senators and many other people answering question after question. Some senators asked Sotomayor questions about decisions she made in cases more than ten years earlier. Sotomayor always answered every question and remembered every case she had heard. Many people praised her work and her

Sotomayor's mother and brother attended the Senate hearings to support her.

abilities to overcome her poor childhood. It may have helped that her mother was sitting right behind her. Celina supported her as she always did.

Some senators still did not think that Sotomayor could be a fair justice. This was because she had once said in a speech that a Hispanic woman would make a better judge than a white man. But Sotomayor met these senators with a smile, saying, "I do not believe any ethnic, racial or gender group has an advantage in sound judgment." She smiled even though the questions were difficult and even though her broken ankle hurt badly because of a poorly fitted cast.

Sotomayor answered questions for hours and hours. She listened to many letters of support written by people whom she had helped. On the final day, witnesses were brought into the Senate. They were asked to discuss Sotomayor's qualifications. They had to explain how she had made a difference in their lives. Even some former Major League Baseball players went to the hearings. They thanked Sotomayor for saving baseball and ending the strike in 1995.

Finally, on August 6, 2009, Sonia Sotomayor was confirmed by the Senate in a 68–31 vote. It was official. The girl from the Bronx would be the first Hispanic Supreme Court justice. When Sotomayor heard the results of the vote, she cried happy tears.

On August 8, 2009, President Obama, the entire Supreme Court, and many others watched as Chief Justice Roberts swore in Associate Justice Sonia Sotomayor. A few days later, President Obama held a big party to present Justice Sotomayor to more than two hundred people at the White House. The president praised Sotomayor's mother for her hard work and her dedication to her daughter's life. President Obama was proud that the U.S. senators had confirmed the first Hispanic Supreme Court justice. He said, "This past Saturday, when Sotomayor was formally sworn in, came yet another step to a more perfect union that we all seek." President Obama also said that Sotomayor had achieved the true American dream, growing up in poverty and rising to the highest court in the entire country.

Life on the Supreme Court

When she was confirmed, Sonia Sotomayor had to move from her office in New York to a new office (called chambers) in the Supreme Court in Washington, D.C. The Supreme Court Building is bigger than any regular courthouse. It includes a law library for the justices, many meeting spaces, stores, a cafeteria, and even a gymnasium for the justices. The basketball court in the gym is often called the Highest Court in the Land, a joke because that is also another name for the Supreme Court.

At the Supreme Court, Justice Sotomayor helps decide some of the most important cases in the United States. The outcome of these cases will affect the freedoms and rights of all Americans. The Supreme Court follows the Constitution to protect all American individuals. It works under the motto Equal Justice Under Law. The Supreme Court's decisions are final. Lower courts must follow its decisions when listening to future cases. Also, the Supreme Court is the only court in the United States from which there is no appeal. This means no other court can hear the case and make a different decision.

Every day, Justice Sotomayor must read many requests from people who want the Supreme Court to hear their cases. These requests are called petitions to grant certiorari, or certs. The Supreme Court normally receives about seven thousand petitions a year to grant cert but usually hears as few as seventy cases each year.

Sotomayor and her family pose on the steps of the Supreme Court Building in September 2009. *Left to right:* stepfather, Omar Lopez; mother, Celina; Sotomayor; sister-in-law, Tracey Sotomayor; and brother, Juan

Doing Justice

Sonia Sotomayor has always cared deeply about making sure that all people in the United States can seek justice. In her college yearbook, she included a quote that said, "I am not a champion of lost causes, but of causes not yet won." When she was at Yale Law School, she filed a discrimination complaint against a law firm that asked her questions about her Puerto Rican background. She wanted to make sure that all employers were fair in deciding whom to hire.

As an appeals court judge, Sotomayor made sure that people were not sent to jail unless they were truly guilty. She decided cases allowing Americans to express their religious ideas. And she made sure that people could get the jobs they wanted, no matter what their race or background—just as she did at Yale Law School.

On the Supreme Court, Sotomayor will decide many cases that may involve women, prisoners, or even people who do not like the United States. When she became a justice, she pledged to "do equal right to the poor and to the rich." As she makes hard decisions, she'll remember that oath, as well as the Supreme Court's motto: Equal Justice Under Law.

To decide which requests to grant, the nine justices read all seven thousand petitions. Then they meet in what is called the conference. During the conference, the justices vote on whether to grant cert and hear the case. If four of the justices vote to grant the petition, then the entire Supreme Court will hear the case.

But Sotomayor's job does not stop there. If the Court grants cert, she must read long documents about the case. These documents are called briefs. They come to the Court from the people whose rights are affected by the case.

Sotomayor joins the Supreme Court justices in this informal photo from September 2009. *Left to right:* Justice Samuel Alito, Justice Ruth Bader Ginsburg, Justice Anthony Kennedy, Justice John Paul Stevens, Chief Justice John Roberts, President Barack Obama, Justice Sotomayor, Vice President Joe Biden, Justice Antonin Scalia, Justice Clarence Thomas, Justice Stephen Breyer, and outgoing justice David Souter

The Supreme Court

The Supreme Court is the highest court in the land. It includes one chief justice and eight associate justices. Each justice has been appointed by the president and approved by the Senate, just as Sotomayor was appointed and approved. Justices serve on the Supreme Court for the rest of their lives, unless they choose to retire early. When a justice dies or retires, the president appoints a replacement.

There are no specific qualifications for becoming a Supreme Court justice. However, the president and Senate must both approve the new nomination. Since 1790 more than one hundred justices have served on the Supreme Court of the United States.

Until 1981 all of these justices were men. But that year, Justice Sandra Day O'Connor *(top right)* was appointed to the Supreme Court. Following O'Connor, Justice Ruth Bader Ginsburg *(bottom right)* became the second woman appointed to the Supreme Court, in 1993. In 2009 Justice Sotomayor became the third female Supreme Court justice. She may well keep in mind the words of Sandra Day O'Connor: "It is most important not to be the last."

Justice Sotomayor and her law clerks read all the briefs in the case. Then they discuss how the case should be decided. A few weeks after the briefs are read, each lawyer in the case comes to the Supreme Court to present his or her side of the argument to the nine justices. During the lawyer's presentation, the justices may interrupt at any time to ask questions. Justice Sotomayor has often asked lawyers difficult questions because the cases affect so many people.

After both sides have made their arguments, the justices meet in a special room to discuss their thoughts about the case. Then each justice writes out an opinion on how to resolve it and passes it around to the other justices. After the justices read and listen to one another's opinions, they take a final vote and make a decision. Supreme Court justices work from October to June every year, and then they have the summers off. For two weeks of most months, they hear the lawyers' arguments and decide which cases to hear. For the other two weeks of most months, the justices often work on writing their opinions.

Life Outside Work

Sonia Sotomayor doesn't work all the time. She also likes to have fun. Family is still very important to her. She enjoys spending time with her brother, Juan, and her niece and twin nephews. Juan is a doctor and university professor in Syracuse, New York. Sotomayor is godmother to five children, and she spends time with them too. She regularly visits her mother and stepfather, Omar Lopez, in Florida. She talks to her mother on the phone every day.

Sonia Sotomayor enjoys being active. She often attends theater and ballet performances. She works out several times a week, usually walking on a treadmill. Sometimes she relaxes at a spa. Sotomayor roots for the Yankees and listens to soft rock music. She puts up fantastic Christmas light displays.

Sotomayor salsa dances with actor Esai Morales at a the annual National Hispanic Foundation for the Arts Noche Musical in Washington, D.C., in 2009.

Finally and perhaps most important, Sotomayor volunteers in the community. She mentors children from poor neighborhoods. She wants to help others achieve their dreams. "I am an ordinary person who has been blessed with extraordinary opportunities and experiences," she has said. "It is this nation's faith in a more perfect union that allows a Puerto Rican girl from the Bronx to stand here now." But, as President Obama has said, "This moment is not just about her. It's about every child who will grow up thinking to him or herself, 'If Sonia Sotomayor can make it, then maybe I can too.'"

FUN FACTS ABOUT SONIA SOTOMAYOR

* She loves tuna fish and cottage cheese for lunch.

* She enjoys the ballet and theater.

* When she goes to Yankee Stadium, she likes to sit in the cheap bleacher seats. People in the bleachers often recognize her.

* She likes soft rock music.

* She has given more than 180 speeches since 1993. About half have been about ethnic and women's issues.

* She enjoys shopping, traveling, and giving gifts.

* She travels to Puerto Rico once or twice a year to visit cousins and relatives who live there.

IMPORTANT DATES

June 25, 1954   Sonia Sotomayor is born in the Bronx, New York

1972   Graduates valedictorian from Cardinal Spellman High School

1976   Graduates summa cum laude from Princeton University

Marries Kevin Noonan

1979   Graduates from Yale Law School

1979–1984   Works as assistant district attorney in Manhattan

1983   Divorces Kevin Noonan

1984–1992   Works as an associate and then partner for the New York law firm of Pavia and Harcourt

1992   Appointed by President George H. W. Bush to be a U.S. district court judge

FURTHER READING

BOOKS

McElroy, Lisa Tucker. *John G. Roberts, Jr.* Minneapolis: Lerner Publications, 2007.

Winter, Jonah. *Sonia Sotomayor: A Judge Grows in the Bronx.* New York: Athenum Books for Young Readers, 2009.

WEBSITES

Ben's Guide to U.S. Government
http://bensguide.gpo.gov/9-12/government/national/scourt.html
This site explains all about the U.S. government, including the Supreme Court and Supreme Court justices.

Congress for Kids: Judicial Branch
http://www.congressforkids.net/Judicialbranch_supremecourt.htm
Check out this site to learn more about the Supreme Court and Supreme Court justices.

INDEX

ACKNOWLEDGMENTS

This book is much better thanks to the interest and excellent research assistance of Ryan Nolan. Ryan, I would not be surprised at all to see you nominated to the Supreme Court one day! Many thanks also go to Mike Barton, Carlos Ramirez, and Tara Clarke for additional research help. To Amy Boss, thanks for being the best mentor on the planet. To Diane Nelson, thanks for supporting this project as you have so many others. To Marcia Marshall, thanks for being a great editor—looking forward to a long working relationship! To Steve McElroy, thanks for being patient, kind, and loving through another one of these. And to Zoe and Abby McElroy, thanks for your great love of reading—this book means so much more because you'll love reading it.